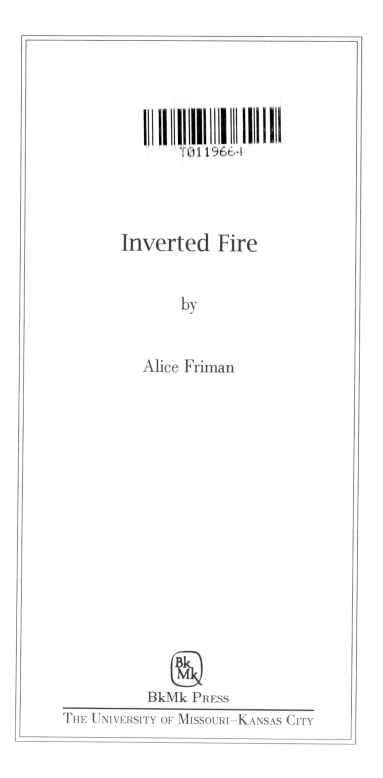

T011966·1

Inverted Fire

by

Alice Friman

BkMk Press

THE UNIVERSITY OF MISSOURI–KANSAS CITY

Also by Alice Friman

Reporting from Corinth
A Question of Innocence (chapbook)
Song to My Sister (chapbook)
Insomniac Heart (chapbook)
Driving for Jimmy Wonderland (chapbook)
Loaves and Fishes: A Book of Indiana Women Poets (editor)

BkMk Press of UMKC
University House
5100 Rockhill Road
Kansas City, MO 64110-2499

Financial assistance for this book has been provided
by the Missouri Arts Council, a state agency.

Cover art by Andrew Hale Illustrations.
Cover design by Brad Kelley.
        E-mail—   coolgrafix@gvi.net
        Internet—   http://home.gvi.net/ ~ coolgrafix/
Interior design by Sherry Sullivan.

Library of Congress Cataloging-in-Publication Data

Friman, Alice.
    Inverted fire / Alice Friman.
        p.   cm.
    ISBN 1-886157-07-3
    I. Title.
PS3556.R5685I68   1997
811'.54--dc20   96-22243
                                                        CIP

Printed in the United States of America on acid-free paper.

10 9 8 7 6 5 4 3 2

Acknowledgments

Some of these poems have appeared in the following publications to which grateful acknowledgment is made.

Abiko Quarterly (Japan), *America, Arts Indiana, Arts Indiana Literary Supplement/Hopewell Review, The Beloit Poetry Journal, Breeze, The Cape Rock, Chelsea, Chester Jones National Poetry Foundation 1991 Anthology, The Cream City Review, Cyphers* (Ireland), *Envoi* (England), *Images, Indiana Review, Iron* (England), *Kentucky Poetry Review, The Laurel Review, MidAmerica, North Dakota Quarterly, Orbis* (England), *Outposts Poetry Quarterly* (England), *Plurilingual Europe* (France), *Poetry Northwest, Poetry Review* (England), *The Prague Revue* (Czech Republic), *PSA News, The Rialto* (England), *Scarp* (Australia), *South Carolina Review, Southern Poetry Review, Staple* (England), *Takahe* (New Zealand), *Tar River Poetry, The Texas Review, Westerly* (Australia), *Writers' Forum, Zone 3.*

"Angel Jewell," "Birthday in Autumn," "Invitation to a Minor Poet," and "Stars" were originally published in *Poetry.*

"Eve," "Flight to Australia," "On Perfection," "Recovery," "Tonight," and "In Neutral" were originally published in *Shenandoah.*

"The Bat" and "Hiking Around Jenny Lake" are reprinted from the *Prairie Schooner* by permission of the University of Nebraska Press. Copyright 1989 by the University of Nebraska Press.

"Love in the Time of Drought, 1988" won the Consuelo Ford Award from the Poetry Society of America, 1988.

"In This Night's Rain" won the Midwest Poetry Award from the Society for the Study of Midwestern Literature, 1990.

"Letter to the Children" won the Cecil Hemley Memorial Award from the Poetry Society of America, 1990.

"Cardiology" won First Prize in the Start with Art Literary Competition sponsored by the Arts Council of Indianapolis, 1992.

"Cherries" won First Prize in the *Abiko Quarterly* International Poetry Contest, Japan, 1994.

Acknowledgment is also made to the following anthologies:

Out of Season: "Angel Jewell," Amagansett Press, 1993; *We Speak for Peace*: "Shame," KIT Publishers, 1993; *Indiannual 4*: "Unposted Letter," Writers' Center of Indianapolis, 1988; *Indiannual 6*: "On Perfection," Writers' Center of Indianapolis, 1992; *What's Become of Eden: Poems of Family at Century's End*: "Walking in Holcomb Gardens," Slapering Hol Press, 1994; *Worlds in Our Words: Contemporary American Women Writers*: "The Good News," Prentice Hall, 1997; *Claiming the Spirit Within: A Sourcebook of Women's Poetry*: "Letter to the Children," Beacon Press, 1996.

The author is grateful to Ragdale, The Virginia Center for the Creative Arts, The Millay Colony for the Arts, Leighton Art Colony in Banff, Canada, and Yaddo, where many of these poems were written. The author also wishes to thank all good friends who have helped over the years with encouragement, advice, and endurance, especially Susan Donnelly, Donald Baker, Roger Pfingston, F. Richard Thomas, Marilyn Kallet, Dale Kushner, and Sandra Adelmund Witt.

Contents

1   Stars

I   Libra

5   Plums
6   Cardiology
7   Snake Hill
8   In This Night's Rain
9   Eve
10   Watching Trees at Steepletop
11   Pigeon Drop
12   Pockets
13   Letter to the Children
15   Journal Entry for Late October
16   Walking in Holcomb Gardens
18   Birthday in Autumn

II   The Moon

23   Flight to Australia, 1989
25   Tonight
26   Love in the Time of Drought, 1988
27   The Shirt
28   On Perfection
29   Callahan's Bride
30   On Loving a Younger Man
31   The Blue Oranda
32   Eurydice's Lot
34   Angel Jewell
35   Shadow
36   A Walk at the End of the Century
37   In Neutral
38   Hiking Around Jenny Lake
40   Northwest Flight #1173

III   Black Hole

43   The Bat
44   Looking for the Parts
45   Sunflowers
46   Unposted Letter
47   Evening in Provence
48   Suppose, Suddenly
49   40° Below
50   Ophelia
52   Rachael Valentine
54   In That Apartment, In That City
55   Riddle
56   Introduction to April
57   Shame

IV   Red Shift

61   Rubber Band
62   Recovery
63   Turnip
64   Invitation to a Minor Poet
65   Letter to My Husband
66   The Good News
68   Archery Lesson
69   Light Years Away
70   Cherries
74   Night Drive

76   About the Author

Inverted Fire

by

Alice Friman

To the children—Richard, Paul, and Lillian—
and, of course, to Bruce

Stars

Heraclitus said
stars are bowls of inverted fire.
In Delos, yes, where they hang from ropes
or Kyparissia, holding up the soft-backed black
like buttons in a love seat. Here
the world's infection makes them dim.

I remember a Greek night,
counting the spread of stars above my head
plus the two broken in his eyes—
a Peloponnesian beach and me
clinging to him, *Alekos*, saying
Alekos, until the moon rose
bleaching the sky tame. Even I
turned alabaster. While behind him, the waves
hunched and groaned under their fallen cargo—
the gleaming crockery of the drowned.

Now, the sky is filled with ghosts:
ashes in the bottom of their bowls
too deep even for the winds
that prowl down the skies sniffing at rims,
howling for a wildness that burns.

I

Libra

All the constellations are animal
or insect except Libra . . . the
balance for weighing the soul.
—Gerald S. Hawkins

Plums

to Bruce

I was a 35-cent child, nothing more.

The silver dollar girl gone
down the slot of all mysteries,
switched for the pale changeling
rocked to awakening in my father's eyes.
Seven years old in the hammock
of my grandmother's yard, I looked up
and saw myself
in the plum-laden branches—sour drupes
of disappointment—and the wry face
and the hand pushing me away.

Admit it. For us the cruelest lesson
was read in a father's eye
or overheard in a voice
coming through a bedroom wall.
And the hardest arithmetic
was subtraction with not enough fingers,
unable to account for the change.

Even you, towering now,
stiffen before your small father
whose only hobby is hoeing his patch,
fingering the fruit of his trees.
We were fed on those juicy knots
of bitterness. Theirs is the jelly
smeared on our morning bread.

Cardiology

In January my sweet gum tree
throws its x-ray against the sky
and last summer's hornets' nest
dangles a heart inside the skeleton.

Everything has a heart.
Tulip bulbs, their one-throb flower.
Plums, a peach. Who knows what membrane
beat in its casing before your prying fingers
stunned the wet slick to stone?
And boulders, too, pushing out from
the ground once every thousand years
when they near their time.

Even the earth.
Big Salty. God's old tart
pulsing yet in the star-stuck, empty ribs.
God's blue forsaken, whose heat still
smokes white at the poles—the continents,
sequins on your dress. Tell me, dear landlady,
tell this child who hides waiting
behind the French doors of a tall emptiness,
put here without provisions
like Gulliver in a strange place, where is
the river leading back—the vena cava to the atrium
where the dark blood loads up for its go-around,
stacking a dawn of red and breathable air?

Snake Hill

to my mother

We are on the final avenue.
Hush now. What's to speak?
Soon we'll go down Snake Hill,
cobblestones and weedy lots.

Will you sing to me as we go?
In the toy store window, the guitar
I wept my heart out for,
the rubber bands still stretched with song.
We can buy it now. There's no end
to what we can afford.
                        I'm lying.
It's gone. The window.
The store. The whole corner where
Frank's Market spilled crates out to the curb.
But I'm still there, wailing,
and you pleading reason to *I want*
I want. (What early prick of glass
keeps that vein open still?)

Snake Hill is steep.
The lyrics overflow the hour. After,
it will take me years to turn
and face that climb alone,
each paving stone weed-wet with song
catching at my throat, my throat
filled with you.
                    Only the child
at the top of the hill
can yank me up again—by the heart's cord
running down the roof of her mouth
to the cut bands of the throat—the child
who has no other choice, having nothing left
from that corner to retrieve.

In This Night's Rain

Like the sacred text
of a mystery religion
thought lost
the trees emerge—wet as birth,
black as the coal of their ancestors.

The white birch that by day
plays with light, curves over
like a ghost
or pallid afterthought.
This night belongs to black.

Not bombazine, buttoned
to the chin over corsets that crack
like bark, but as your mother was,
dressed in shadow at the corner of your bed,
beating down terror by breathing—a presence
before light and beyond
that returns tonight
to stand in this deep immensity,
this black bath that was once its air.

Questions tap at my umbrella.
A white cat crosses my path.

On a night like this, Oedipus
walked to face the questioner
who asked the easiest riddle in her book
because she too loved his too-proud eye.

Yes, a night like this, and a tree
like this, rising in its robe of shadow—
the familiar scent beside him
in the dark—dripping from its tips
a warning of love's black first milk.

Eve

from a sculpture by Rodin

She walked into his coils
as one wades into velvet drapery
embracing the heavy folds, one leg

through to the other side. The rest of her
stayed inert in the slow-moving spiral
that slid like time across her eyes.

Somewhere on the outside she heard
a question and in her answering thought
knew that this was paradise.

When the other one left
with his hymns and obscene whispers
she kissed both hands to the sky.

What could she understand of "Daddy" and
"begetting," what of the peacock's tail
trailed hissing in the weeds? Destruction

cracked outside the gates, glittered
behind the owl's placid eye. The mouse
staggered in her hand. She swerved.

Much later, after the other one was gone
and all you've come to know about
had passed, her heart knocked again

in hunger and she went back. They fed
on apricots and figs and, smaller now,
he coiled in her lap, then, remembering,

spoke in braille the enameled story of
his skin, sloughing it off in the telling.
She hung it like a mural from the tree.

The cock preened and crowed. And from
between two rocks, the thorns
bloomed like teeth.

Watching Trees at Steepletop

at Edna St. Vincent Millay's farm

In a straight line up the hill
from the writer's cabin door,
three trees, twenty feet apart
as if they climbed. She must
have sat—the big green chair,
paper, pen, a book to lean on—
staring and imagining a fourth,
a fifth: a long line marching
like a parade beyond the limits
of the ridge: a rope of birds
to her imagined "South." Or did
she watch the flies bump frantic
against the screens as if they
too could see the trees? (That
morning's three become a buzzy
five—the next day's carcasses
on the sill.)
        In my parents' house
a plastic ailanthus fills the
empty space, removed from pain,
indifferent to the sun that like
a spotlight or a golden rooster
pecking seed gladdens the valleys
of the rug. Six days a week my
mother wipes it with a rag—dusts
the raised limbs, their feathery
ends, the numbed notion of its
stillness: the untouched, blood-
less kiss. On the 7th day she
rests, her big green chair next to
her life—laid brick on brick—
a wall or ridge. What will save
her if the tree of heaven's ill
and imagination, like a flower,
has been knifed off at the knee?

Pigeon Drop

from a first line by Carolyn Kizer

At a party I spy a handsome psychiatrist
next to the dip on the edge
of the sofa. He's stroking his socks,
his ankles too thin for his body.
I'm tempted to ask advice, what to do
about Mother and the father I've not spoken to
for ten years who can barely get out of his chair,
who falls in the parking lot outside Burdine's
on the way to the summer sale of walking shorts
he'll never wear. It's not I'm afraid he'd say
call your father, write, extend a hand. He'd never—
knowing. It's his ankles, too trim, crossed
over like that, the socks too black, too new,
as if he'd just bought them, maybe at Burdine's,
whistling out the double glass doors, across
the lot to the red Buick, too young and shatterproof
to figure out that man over there, inching his walker,
the grip, the line of the mouth, for 87 years the eyes
darting—old bird in the eaves, looking around
for where to drop.

Pockets

In my father's pocket
bits of tobacco and the handkerchief
he hacked in, the one Mother boiled
on Monday morning's stove. But no child.
She fell out the bottom through the hole
he plucked at, kept ragged with his nail
so she could get back in, crawling
up his leg to do it again, hanging on
to the shredded edges as if life depended on it.

Sugar in a spoon: white dirt
dumped in his morning coffee.

Every child has a father who is king,
a straight-backed decree with a strut.
Some children have a father who is God.

Sometimes I hear my old choirs singing
in my hair in their stiff white dresses.
Old cells, old saints' lives,
old hymns inventing his tinny love.

Now I have inherited my father's pockets.
Lady of grand gesture, sweeper of statements
who can hold on to nothing, who plucks
at her seams that once every five years
must be stitched up with scar.

Only in the pocket of my new blue coat
do I save things—a dolly's arm,
a plastic yellow dog—toys picked up in gutters
lost from a child's stash. I call them messages, each
another chance before the family disease
eats away the lining. I finger them as I walk—
proxies, my treasures in braille,
my joeys in a pouch, feeding where they're warm
and, for a while, wanted.

Letter to the Children

In the new cold of late September
the prongs of Queen Anne's lace that held
their doilies up like jewels
rise then stiffen, crushing toward center,
making wooden enclosures to die in
like the ones the Celts built to hold their enemies
then set aflame. The goldenrod leans,
licks at their cages. And all that's left of daisies
are burnt-out eyes.

I walk these back fields
past the swish of cattails in their silver
grasses, the old ones
showing the woolly lining of their suede jackets
while the thistle, dried to gray,
bends her trembling head
and spills her seed.

It is the time—the great lying-in of Autumn—
and I am walking its wards.
And I remember it was now, late September
then on into the deep gully of fall—when the hackberry
groans and the black oak strains in its sockets, the winds
pushing in the long forest corridors—
that I too was born and gave birth.

And you are all Autumn's children, all
given to sadness amid great stirrings
for you were rocked to sleep in the knowledge
of loss and saw in the reflection outside your window,
beyond the bars of your reach, your own face
beckoning from the burning promise
that little by little disappeared. What can I give you
for your birthdays this year, you who are the match
and the flaming jewel, whose birthright consumes itself
in the face of your desire?

If you were here with me now
walking down this day's death,
I would try to show you two things: how the last light
plays itself out over the thistle's labors,
over the wild cherry heavy with fruit, as if comfort
lay in what it had made. And how that black bird
with flame at his shoulders
teeters for balance on a swaying weed.

Journal Entry for Late October

This morning
fog tucks in like a sheet.
Everything outside is still. The trees
are concentrating on their business of
letting go—leaves, acorn, hickory—down
straight and fast. The forest is hollowing out.
All that's left are mysteries.

On a rotten log
lines of fungi: a thousand
pink nipples pressed close and
rubbery as erasers. I run my finger
over the perfect rows in wonder the way I once saw
an elephant run her trunk's delicate tip
hesitantly, gingerly, over another's death,
wag her head, leave, come back
to do it again.

It is the seeing touch of a blind eye
groping for the water in the rock
before the crack and gush, or the tap
of the hazel, brushed lightly
over the face in the mirror
to release the bride.

It is the touch of awe—the knowledge
born in the fingertips and pulled
by the thing itself—the uneasy finger
scouting for what the hand has yet to learn:

Once I saw a tree, six hands around, twisted
back and away from its indifferent half,
grown from the same root. Not struck down
straight, but arching like a woman racked,
the belly split, the secret insides rumbling out
black in scallops. I waded through brambles
and unseen mud to touch it, to run
a finger along its gaping hole
where the heavy woodiness had boiled out like scar.

Walking in Holcomb Gardens

to my mother

Let's say we choose what we take in
not from want or even need
but from something left undone
(paint cans on the floor   paper never hung
dreams woken up too soon).

Two rose-pinked mushrooms.
This great red oak.
A silver butterfly preening on my thumb.

Six hands around couldn't latch this puzzle closed.

Mushrooms. Butterfly. Oak.
Rune stones flung together.
The spell of a witch's brew

and once more
steam fills the kitchen on Wadsworth Avenue
from handkerchiefs boiling on the stove,
from clouds in a pot of starch, and you,
plying the yellow soap on Monday's board,
rub again at all our weekly sins,
twisting your arms, wringing
through the lines of your hands
what last wet remains in a cotton blouse.

I sit at the table swinging my legs
eating the egg sandwich you fixed
between the last rinse and the bluing
adoring you like Cinderella's child

and then
as from a castle's secret wall
you step out from the forbidden door
you dressed behind in your good black dress,
its square neck spread low and faced with satin.

The pillow flesh dipping in and out of its
own dizzy crease, trembling in the spotlight
of a pair of rhinestone clips, so beautiful—
so rare, this bow to the flesh

we cheeped around you like your birds.

Today, walking across this expanse
of lawn I hear the trains blow from
some distant place pulling freight
up impossible hills. Two thousand miles
away, you come tugging at my memory,
flashing for my attention wherever I look.

Mama, what's been left undone?
Where's the door we didn't close?
What silver child never grown
comes through now
fluttering at my fingers?

I lean against this red oak
whose rich vertical heart has pulled water
for over four hundred years and must know.

What dream needs finishing? what story told?
Whose child rocks her forehead
against this rough and silent tree
weeping for her mother?

Birthday in Autumn

At 4 o'clock
October tips her light
in low through any west window
and a dirty cup holds
in some forgotten sink
a sun spot
to the curve of its tea.

Now more than any other time
should cold and heat weigh each other
out and the balance beam level: the promise
holding its own against the graying hairs.

Yet when October comes
carrying gold in its slotted spoon,
as if she bid me feed on what runs
streaming out, I'm not fast enough
and clamp my teeth on an empty spoon.

What is the message
but to put aside the shudder
of finality—this dying animal
that has carried me like a crown
through tangled streets, the inevitable
white-haired bone—so the harvest
can pour itself into its baskets,
sheer and gold?

October 20
and once more the wild gift:
ribbons of birds,
a rustle of generosity,
the dancing drift of bread.
I should grow fat on such manna.
But all I see are arms
like half-forgotten selves, stretching

in their raveling blouses, thin and
delicate as a young girl's again,
to take November when he comes
in all his privilege,
in all his icy heat.

II

The Moon

No other heavenly body except
meteors ever comes this close to us.
—Arthur M. Harding

If she is fire, the moon has all
the more need of earth . . . on which
she stands and to which she clings.
—Plutarch

Flight to Australia, 1989

Flying backwards
into the day after tomorrow
I think—this perpetual night—
of the invisible curve
we cling to, each in our ten-seat-across
row, huddled in blankets
balancing the cup
buttering the roll: the curve
that holds us to what matters: schedules,
children, the one in the yellow sweater
who kissed and clutched me goodbye.

The group from Vantage Tours
wear blow-up pillows around their necks,
name tags with stars.
They settle to sleep in tandem
as if they learned how from a manual.
The men from Lennox Furnace
talk of blowers and last year's
week in Rio when sales were high.
They flip the pages of their magazines,
adjust their bellies for the long haul. Their wives
lean back delicately.

In Honolulu where we stop, less
than a third of the way there, we gather
at the bathroom mirror, eye each other
warily under the fluorescent tubes,
brush our teeth, our hair, and try
to make up again the face
behind which we make up the world.

How many dinners can we eat? how many
bad movies can be swallowed down before
we grow fuzzy again, run our tongues
over our teeth, grunt in an alien sleep?

Twenty hours between sunset and rise, the limbs
ache for the old familiar parent, not this
stepmother of discomfort who
straps us to her like guilt.
Who was it buried the dead sitting up in a narrow box?

Outside, the moon stretches back,
grins in her wide black bed.

This unnatural sleep reminds us
of the other, but when *that* comes
who will care enough to mind?
It's life that is uncomfortable,
sets the heart to ache, makes us,
like a ten-month pregnancy,
strain the confines of even good intentions.

Even the members of Vantage Tours
begin to struggle against their straps.
No pillow of comfort
can soften the news outside this cabin window:
The moon has disappeared.
The stars are fixed in disinterest.
And anywhere beneath the distraction of our own noise
a shark wakes and cruises in the corrugated sea.

Tonight

Tonight the moon is eating her own shadow.
Soon she will grow fat
and light both hemispheres with her loneliness.
She will become all belly with it
then begin to waste away.
And every full-lipped child
who's discovered its own slipping heart,
whose sleep has circled around
the dream of broken things,
is caught in her mirrored wheel.
No comfort of dolly or blue-ribboned hat,
no red-stitched leather ball,
can break that old waxed round.

Year after year, even by day,
she leans in her white make-up
to gather in her own: riding the bus,
teaching a class, their lips pale
as linen flowers, two crescents
on either side where she has placed
her cold hands, cupping the O O O
of their loneliness. See them in their
grown-up skins staring out windows
or in Chicago or New York, waiting for her
to reach through the concrete netting,
as she always does,
pulling at them with her moody eyes.

Love in the Time of Drought, 1988

Only at the movies do we slide in,
our elbows on the armrest
then the upper arms
hinging us like the cylinder of a lunar moth:
two wings breathless on either side.
You sigh and then an imperceptible groan
as if you were haunted all your life
by this. I look at your face.
You are studying the coming attractions,
afraid there'll be a test.

Look, this summer the only fire
waiting to happen is in the fields, so dry
cows cut their tongues and Queen Anne's lace
swallows down like pride.
Besides, my old insomniac heart
is chained to its army cot. Watch the movie.

It's a story about Rome in a wet July and
two lovers arm in arm on the Ponte Sant' Angelo
where from the railing Bernini's wind-
whipped angels watch their eyes out blind.
The rain comes down like tears.

I am too old for feeble episodes
in lock-step order. I want what angels miss
in their pale heaven that makes them
come down, ecstatic in drapery, to stand,
hands out and empty, crying in the rain.

The Shirt

I've hung it on the closet door—
your black shirt. The space your chest
and back pushed out falls lonely now
as if it had forgotten the slow beating
heart, the heft of your shoulder, the great
wall of your back. Still, I could not
hang it in the closet with the other things
that I unpacked—shaking them out
like so many folded days—not even
the white blouse I wore our last night
that would have recognized its smell—
its own white shadow—still stirring
against the black fastenings.

If I have taken myself away, piling
the miles up between us—we who have
such distances already—you should know
that now in this little room of white
painted furniture, of curtains
parted and pulled back like my hair
when I was young, I have tried to put
everything neatly in its place, maybe
to find again an older space from
some imagined morning of a life—
a simpler light, perhaps, that never was.
Yet I couldn't bring myself to put away
this black ghost of you—soft from
too many washings, clinging to its black
as if it were a right, like a thing
one has to earn and learns to keep private
in a world demanding to be compromised.

Last night I wore it while I slept.
The yardage, so used to holding
your chest, folded itself down
to cup this flesh that you had loved
through a night of imperfect dreams.

On Perfection

On the day we went to Toronto
    to eat stuffed derma
and shop for a Persian rug
    you said, crossing the street,
that Lear always made you cry,
    the way before he died
he pleaded "undo this button." Such
    a simple thing, the perfection
of that line, like the rug of
    glowing color sudden
on the shop floor when we were leaving
    as if it were not there
when we came in although bells rang
    both times to tell us so.
Yet you laugh at me, saying it's I
    who crave perfection—the
four-leaf in a wealth of three—as if
    perfection were the oddity
in an ordinary world of clover and not
    all around us: the base,
the origin, the underlying point
    that bleeds the heart's wish
then twists it—a barbed wire—through
    the censorship of our days
to save us. All else is empty talk
    to fill a lecture hall.
Don't you remember the long night-
    ride home when we each sat
shrunken into the corners of ourselves
    in that big car, desperately
filling with words the space between us—
    the space, simple and perfect,
clanging out its emptiness like a bell?

Callahan's Bride

Callahan painted shamrocks on the mailbox
then went at the woods with a backhoe
to give her a lawn
tight around the house like a ring.
From the kitchen window, hands busy with garden
radish and strawberry—bite-sized hearts
he'd examine for imperfections—she watched
the trees sway like bridesmaids
catching at the sun's last flung light.

In the beginning when he was gone
she'd walk the back roads—apple in a pocket
humming in her mouth—stop at the trestle
to wave in his evening train, its five blue cars.

But last October when the fog
dragged its veils along the forest floor,
feverish she went among the trees, greeting one
then another as if pressing cheek to cheek and
they in turn reached out a yellow touch
or brushed her with a chartreuse glove. Two maples
bowed and offered trays of reds, and she,
as if she had to choose, hung in white between them,
startling as birch or a pear tree made of glass.

On Loving a Younger Man

One day when I am 91
you will look at me from the doorway, leaning
with your head tilted to one side
and I will wonder if you remember
how I too used to lean
and lay my hair down black and whispering on the
pillowcase fresh from the wash, or how
later I would turn
tucking my knees under yours
for the night's insensible hours.
     And if I haven't forgotten—my mind
gone blank as a sheet—I'll remind you then
of the old amazed look your face wore once
at how much your hands already knew,
and I will call you back
from the doorway
to adjust the sweater around my shoulders,
the robe in my lap, and take your hand, upturned
in mine, to show you how that line is still there:
the life line I once traced with my nail,
that day on the bench by the Ohio River, that first
time, when I—troubled—leaned my head on your shoulder,
sideways, the way I do now
and you will then.

The Blue Oranda

We bought her because she was blue-
silver as my wedding dress
and beautiful two months ago
holding roses to my face
with you so happy
we were sure they'd never fade.

Today she's dying.
We stand over her bowl.

Round and around the bottom shells her veils drift,
sheeting silver off as did my grandmother's
silver-plated spoon I keep to remind me
how it once held honey and glanced through tea.

We cheer her efforts to right herself,
adjust our breathing to the panic of her gills.

More is at stake here than
another Pisces daughter going down in veils.
We are afraid of omens: a rose-hip fortune
read from faded cups, or worse, much worse—
the gauzy spell, the silver glance,
the head brought in on Wednesday's common plate.

Eurydice's Lot

He packed it up—
the camel, the tasseled rugs,
the copper pots clanking off the hump—
leaving the old girl behind, veiled to the spot,
two feet jammed into one shoe.

Couldn't carry a tune
or tweedle a pipe but hero enough he'd be
to lead Eurydice out if he'd a mind to,
not giving a damn, the way he did,
if she fell or followed. One eye he had
and that forward, forward,
straight to Duluth if he knew
where that was, not that
it would have mattered in a world
where looking back with sorrow
for what never was is worse
than following a camel's rump
anywhere it goes.

And Eurydice? Mama's apple girl?
She'd have trudged behind
squinting for a sudden sign or stir,
crooning for the sly one
to come in from the high grass again
winding his surgeon's eye
the way he did that first time
when love-stiffened he coiled
then nibbled her soft into sweet brown sin:

"Oh, Worm
Great Slitherer
hammer of my heel
of my heel's own heart

Subtlety of double sight
in whose salt rings
all future spins, and past,
the same as what that other
must have seen—cocoon of sorrows,
prisoner of her own salt-spun eye

Here in front of me—single file—
shuffles dry duty
a different kind of cage

Sweet Vicious
Shucker of Skins
come and help me now."

Angel Jewell

I give you the end of a golden string
Only wind it in a ball,
It will lead you in at Heaven's gate
Built in Jerusalem's wall.
                                        —Blake

Was it the fatal perfection of her name
that sent her among us, so thin
the veins showed in her finger tips?
Skin drawn tight as cellophane
was window on a painting we couldn't bear to see.
Her eyes were blue, too large. Her hair
a cirrus cloud. She lived on air.

What had she to do with what we were—
jostling our corn-fed shoulders, hefting
our packs, our books, our good red laughs?
And of the attentive earth—
the slant barn roof,
the Holstein's swaying bag,
the worm-churned dirt that works the seed,
wraps the root and pushes out the food—
what had she to do with that?
From the beginning she was heaven's freight.

We must have known before she left.
Why didn't we gather then
to press in her pocket as she passed
or in her hand, a note on onionskin
or other weightless thing—the way they stuff
the cracks in Jerusalem's ancient wall
with wailing or a plea?

Shadow

The morning sun leaps blue
spreading at our feet the imprint
of its gift: our blowing hair
cloudy across a crosswalk
then mingled with the grass.

You glance at where I point,
clutching book and papers,
determined to hold tight the day's intentions.
I see myself in the shield of your eyes.

I think of Medusa, sun at her back,
waiting at the rock-edge of exile,
how she leaned to her floating shadow, the hair
impatient in the hissing foam.
And when he came—hero, crooning
as if he were the sun's own emissary—calling her
from her one comfort, she turned and saw
in the single mind of his retina, the stare of quartz:
the face love cannot look upon and live.

She bent her head back for the sword.

Sometimes when we walk, our shadows
cross over, blend, then separate—whole again—
unlike us who when we part must haul away
the stone of one another's eye.

I wish two-equals-one were a simpler arithmetic,
the way it is at dawn when the night's shadow
leaves our room, and we (less flesh than light)
float like two planets across her palms.

A Walk at the End of the Century

Last night in the southwest quadrant of the sky,
a light, low and yellow, too bright for planet or star.
It glowed. It lit the clouds. I said it was the moon
reduced—the last dot phase before dying. You laughed.
A new astronomy for a new age. And we both thought
of the fat-cheeked face of our old comfort peeking
in the car playing now-you-see-me-now-you-don't through
trees, forgetting who in its high white wig of bone
points *j'accuse* through our bedroom window. We walked.

And except for talk of strange light where the moon's
last crescent should have been, we spoke of news and
the French doctor's face in East Africa who knelt
holding his hands over a huddle of bones like a boy scout
feeling for fire in an arrangement of sticks—this pencil,
an arm, this, a thigh, and that swollen knob, the skull,
eyes drilling from the holes. I know. It goes on goes on,
something about cycles. But tell me—

When Death's head is screwed onto a child, easy
as a light bulb, how do beginning and end come full circle
and not add up to zero? And how can a body, eaten down to laser
or probe of light, be bright enough for conscience but not cure?

In Neutral

The moon puts down a foot
and the sea marches
white shakos to the shore.
A tree reaches its toes underground
thinned to hollow hairs
sucking   sucking. Only I
have no obsessions, no clutch
at the nape, no slam against the wall.

I rummage the kitchen drawer
for long thin things, the rope,
the cord, the bakery string that would
leap from my hand and suspend me in wonder,
become my green inevitable,
my cannot-help-it, my swoon.

At night I walk as far as the basswood
raining seed like D-Day parachutes
over Rouen, twirling in and out
of searchlights, not dead yet
but dead weight in the cords.
I walk with my head down.
I have become professor of sidewalks,
the accountant of lost coin, prophet
of cracks, a lamppost with a broken neck:

A peacock who trailed his glory up a hill,
then lay down on his side so the wind
could lift the long blue hair
and all its eyes could watch himself sleeping.

Hiking Around Jenny Lake

Grand Teton National Park

> in nature there are few sharp lines: there are areas
> —A. R. Ammons

Here is nature for surgeons—a country of straight
lines, cones and geometry. Sixty-foot pines,

up and unbending, or stripped by weather, fallen
in shining poles of silver, level or slant.

Purple asters horizontal on their stems. A thistle
flashing violet, upright as a stop sign. On the west

side of this lake I walk, the mountains rise like a maxim.
Behind them the sun slips down each night, sometimes

clutching at their tops to hold on longer, but the sides,
too sheer and stony hard without a tree to stop them,

will not give her half an inch past her time.
Of birth? The rocks scrape up beneath my feet

sharp already in their edges and every month the moon
pushes out again to fill her cold circumference.

And because summer comes, quick past and done,
there is no time for vines to wrap the trees

against the winter and no time for betrayal when
bodies turn against themselves and bend, softening

into their own dying. Nothing to turn my head
away from. Nothing faint. Nothing to be forgiven.

At night, a light wind reaches up under my blankets
to carry the warmth away while the stars go about

their business and the Snake River, chilled to
silver in the moonlight, races past my door.

Here stands the diorama of perfections: the answers
at the back of the geometry book without the problems.

How can one think here except in straight lines?
The mountains' silhouette—sometimes shrouded, sometimes

backlit against the haze—yet the same. If changed
not in my lifetime or a thousand. Is this the easy way?

Choosing to see lines instead of spaces? Or is it
that each place we walk evokes another paradigm of being

already tucked in our own gray folds: all the infinite
scapes of the world: Ammons' "areas of primrose," his

"disorderly orders of bayberry," and this pristine subjection
where even the bull elk are pulled like sleepwalkers

into the meadow's August rectangle, to raise their heads,
paw at the obedient ground, and bugle lovingly for their cows.

Northwest Flight #1173

We guessed your silent passage
by the phosphorescence in your wake.
At dawn we found you stranded on the rocks.
—Stanley Kunitz

We sit on the tarmac in Indianapolis.
Four hours, five, punctuated by coffee
and too small cakes on miniature trays.
The rain taps at the rows of little windows—
the only recognition from the outside world
that we are there—while we,
like the ark on drizzling Ararat,
wait for the levels to go down: the generators
to work. I read poetry and think of whales.
A beached body, its grunts and squeaks,
small tracks like the flashing instrument panel
that measures the dying of a great interior.

I remember last August when I saw one
trailing phosphorescence off Provincetown:
the long languorous arc of the body dipping
in and out like a needle hemming the seas,
while circling birds above the blowhole
announced the repeated baptism of tonnage,
the metamorphosis of breath to rainbow.

Transferred to another plane, rocking at last
on the runway, all windsocks go, the great wings
spread out over their humming eggs of energy,
we lift, shuddering through fog, to where the sun
pumps above our small geometric lives, and I
wonder as we climb, buoyant in our blindness,
if we too want—like a silver needle freed
of thread—entrance into insubstantial air.

III

Black Hole

Outside the black hole space and
time are normal, but inside they
are not.
                —Gerald S. Hawkins

a black hole . . . the set of events
from which it [is] not possible to
escape
                —Stephen W. Hawking

The Bat

A siren wails away the day
and all murderous intent
shuffles off to bed.
What sweet baby talk
lays us down
that over our roof, our pillow,
the night will grind its wheel
while we—all star lights on—sleep
safe in its parking lot: tomorrow
everything sure to come back
to where we left it? Then what
was the scream I pulled down
last night from the blind beating air,
smothered and stomped flat on the
blue carpet, grinding with my heel?
What was the innocent spot
oozed from its mouth that all
my scrubbing only makes brighter,
but the inner flash of a bluer wilder
spot that like a throw rug on a carpet,
like the day's own blue face, fails to hide
the irredeemable black hole?

Looking for the Parts

In Ireland I feel I may find my soul,
and in London next fall, my brain, and
maybe in heaven what was my heart.
                              —Sylvia Plath

In the mean time of a life, all the parts—
strung together on their blue wires,
standing their watch,
minding their own business—seem lost.
To the numb one they stand around like cut
flowers at a wake or statues with empty eyes.

The sun goes down, goes down, goes down.

Was it yesterday you found your face
stretched out on the back of a spoon?
the insides of your heart heaped
like sand in the sugar bowl?

What difference then—
the seasons unzipping themselves,
the spring's dark billy-goat song?

Something else has decided to live,
something in the wall between you
and the woman who lives next door,
the one who's never home to hush the baby
whimpering in your sleep—something
behind the lathing, deaf as a turnip,
bitter as radish, its white root hairs
inching down between the walls, groping
toward the worm-churned rescuing dirt.

Sunflowers

France, 1990

As we pass
their faces turn to the drama
which is us, not the sun:
a field of caution lights on a hillside
in their best frilled paper caps.

They do not watch the sun,
that's another fable,
but turn away
keeping shyness in unison.
They are girls bowing green necks
too young for the golden wimple, their inevitable
weight: they are saints *before* their lives,
before the voices and the post, the calling
and the consummation in a flame dress.

We cross the Rhône heading south,
pass field after field of them watching us
and remember another
who, trembling under their gaze, lowered
a dozen into a jar of cool water, then took
their heavy heads into his hands because
he saw—as in a self-portrait—the coming terror
of their one huge burnt-out eye.

Unposted Letter

Yesterday, walking the meadows at dusk
I watched the colors drain themselves down
like some voluntary graying of the fields.
Then the daisies—white palms up—
clicked on like prophecy and I thought I heard
the rabbits howling in the warrens like the lost.

Lieutenant, I am afraid. Wild roses
fold themselves down at dusk, one could
wade these fields calling, swiping at the weeds
never to find them. Only in my dream
do the colors still come—your cheek,
a tangle of wild roses on my pillow.

Oh, do not misunderstand.
I have my own room of walls and every day
a white egg on a white plate. But where
will I go when I cannot tell the difference
between my face and the moon's? between my hands
and the white twisted napkin knotted in my lap?

Last night in the field, the daisies, flashing
white enamel, snapped their fingers—*No*
they said, *No*. Their yellow eyes, like the last
yellow in my morning egg, broken
and running down the sides.

Evening in Provence

In the book of Claudine
a window wider than all outdoors
opens each day on the same page
where a towered bell
wags its evening tongue over
red-tiled roofs
and pigeons slowly scoop up the sky
arcing like the crescents
of a young moon's double horn.

Claudine runs her hands through her hair
leans against the sill
trying to unbraid the evening—
to put the roses back into the garden,
the pigeons, head-hiding, back under eaves,
not insisting through her shuttered
louvres this oppressive loveliness she's
forced to fling wide to each evening
and meet with a bell-echoing heart.

In the book of Claudine
paint the flowers in her window box
so bright they might break.
They're planted there for proxy.

Suppose, Suddenly

Suppose, suddenly you're locked
in a telephone booth with a slasher.

The little life you watered like a petunia
caught in that stand-up coffin
smelling of shopping bags and urine.

You yell and bang at the glass.
People turn and stare, wagging their heads
too heavy for their necks,
the door shuddering, dead on its own hinges.

You try to get away
but he's there, swiping at your collar,
using up all the air

waving the flat of the blade
slowly at your throat
like a hypnotist's watch, his eyes

flashing pieces of your life
like old black and white glossies
down the nickel and dime slots of the phone.

And suddenly you realize
this is it—the gleaming edge from which
the past and future slice away like bread—
what the glass eye of the fox
biting its own tail was waiting for:

the cutting edge *always* curled around your neck,
always ran in the seam of your collar
along the string of your mother's pearls.

Your life never was
more than a smudge on the side of a blade
that could be wiped off with a rag.

40° Below

that New Year's Eve and the
trains moving into Germany
                    —Lillian Hellman

When Fahrenheit and Celsius,
tracked and locked in numbers, meet,
like long-lost relatives thought dead
(an experiment perhaps on the effects
of cold on the human body)—or worse:

two trains running side by side
but never together, mother and daughter
frantic for each other's face, to know
for that moment the other lives
(would leap life for that) and then
at last to reach out and grab on
before the fingers slipping, before
the hurtling to (who can imagine)
such showers and such heat.

Ophelia

That Sunday nothing big moved.
Only flies. Ticks. Beetles.
Things that nibble and saw.
Gnats flying in hosts.
Dragonflies who dip a double wing
then drop to hover and watch.

All Elsinore. The cows.
The ghost. The rest. Heavy with heat.
Why else would she choose
water for her sleep?

She lay down easy, easy
as leaning back on a castle's
secret wall. She wasn't afraid.
Around her beetles walked on water
coupling like saints to their own image
then gathered to her side
to twirl like dervishes
on the cool reflection of her sheets.
She floated, drifting and turning—
an abandoned boat, dripping
rings from her fingers. Her hair
unbraiding, spreading out like weed.

The sun flashed an S O S.
But she, half in half out,
surrendered to that wet cloister
the sound of her own heart held safe
in the wimple of water around her face.
She and her reflection consummated at last
in the lapping of that nunnery.

She leaned back into the water
as one presses into the side of sleep,
then turned her head
to kiss herself good night.

The dragonflies watched
twisting their pea-green heads,
zoomed down on double wings
to pick and pluck their feed.
One lit on the bodice of her dress
and preened. Overhead, an oriole
flashed his beauty to hold her.

Under her, the water tilted
and swung open.

Rachael Valentine
1978-1993
for Flora

Outside the synagogue
the low sun cast our shadows
waiting in line at the threshold.
We were nothing but air, a trick of light
come to fill the hole no dirt could.

How each heart-cracked moment
arrives with its attendant image.

Her name meant *beloved*.
But to us who never knew, hadn't come
to recognize how her ways differed
from those of any girl just out of braces,
what could we say?

We came because she was yours,
because this day was named, called out
from the meager cash crop of the rest,
for you to put her down.

What measures this?
Who dares the red-soaked prize?

For the heart that gives and gives
to be shrunken inside a pencil case
adrift in the desk of a child who'll never
return to her homework—the vocabulary of it,
the subtraction, subtraction—oh, how
does a heart erase its own blueprint
and rebuild itself into a fortress, an icehouse?

Mother, whose name conjures flowers,
silence the fool who'd instruct you.

You asked for words.
I give you back the one you gave to her.
Her name meant *beloved*. Now take it home
for the cut in your chest that will
gape and close, gape and close—
the hurt accordion sawing its whywhywhy.

In That Apartment, In That City

Why did she do it—thump
crazy on his chest to bring him back?
What instinct was it—it couldn't
have been thought—to return him
to the shredder where morphine
cannot even rock *itself* to sleep?

You couldn't call it a child's wish
that so briefly dead
he could still be grabbed back
like a letter from the slot
before the black kiss of cancellation,
or denied the ferry, not having
the correct coin, or Lazarus amazed, up
in his chair again without the sores.
She was beyond all that.

And how is it now for her who loved him
to have watched him wrestled down, lion-
clawed, and stomach eaten away
before the snap of the jugular
not after, so that
by the time he groaned, still at last,
she lost the name of the enemy
and ran, dragging him back
into the jaws and roiling tongue
that sleep now
slack-open in her unforgiving bed.

Riddle

for Margo

Yesterday she let me touch your bones,
showing her last three years
in a gesture. The life she carried
in dying, in death, shook out in my hand
from a fuchsia vial, glitter and
iridescent stars mixed in with the pieces
whitened in fire and rough as gravel—
some big as the fingernail I poked in first,
slowly as though I were three again in icing.

Can you forgive a stranger, touching
what no one who ever loved you could,
what the flesh hid, white-naked
in its jealousy, laying itself alongside
and trembling around? I told her it felt
as if I held your heart but that was my own
talking, marking quick time in its lockup.

Who are you to have become so
light and remote as bath salts in a jar
or a child's handful of broken shell
loosely poured from one palm to another
then left on the back porch step come September?
Who, if not what the sea is looking for,
thrashing in its salty memory, each time
it crawls up on land, banging at the slanted door.

Introduction to April

Without the heft of love
Or other shadows dragging at my heel

The magnolia spreads out her glory
Robins dive-bomb the new lawns

Without meaning.
For the story

There should be a deaf person
Positioned in the corner

To spell out lovely with her hands
Like these magnolia blossoms

Falling
That above all

Nothing matters but that we make it up.
We have to. There are such empty spaces

Between the spread wings
The rush of air

The worm struggling in the tidy machinery.

Shame

March 1991

> And yellow was the multiplying sand
> —Dylan Thomas

1.
Now in the pre-ornamental spring
ice-covered ruts thaw underfoot
and puddles open up like eyes. What
does the water see before it disappears
to make it fall on us again like rain?

2.
It is the wrong season.
It's Xmas we want. And snow.
Snow to block windows, to freeze
shut the eyes of water. Snow
in high drifts packed snug against
the house. Not flurries but storms,
snows of ribbons, blizzards of ribbons,
one hundred and fifty thousand sleet-
blinding yellow ribbons to decorate
the axed trees of bone, to camouflage
the stiff packages of flesh, to cover
the coffins that insist on being counted,
crawling up out of the sand.

How many miles of the stuff
can we manufacture? How much taffeta?
Grosgrain? Curl-with-a-scissor acetate?
How many bobbins? It will take
nine yards to wrap around each box—
each gift of grief—plus
the two feet necessary for a bow
and we'll need plenty left for lapels,
corsages, wreaths, plenty to sell Boy Scouts

and beer, to wrap trees and a streak
of yellow over our eyes.

3.
We have added death to death
and call it a clean new arithmetic
with no word for subtraction.

A general is our new sex symbol.
He holds up his pants with ribbons.
He loops up his fly with ribbons.
He wishes codpieces were fashionable.

Even God is decorated: his skull
lacing yellow in and out
the sockets of his eyes: God
of maggot and the shame of angels
waving his yellow banner
in front of his television—
rooting for the home team.

4.
In the desert
the sweet yellow ribbons
of the body's fat are melting
—yellow, yellow is the multiplying sand.

We have broken decency on the wheel
and are teaching the children to flutter
their little flags in the endless procession.

IV

Red Shift

The size of a galaxy's red shift is . . .
directly proportional to the galaxy's
distance from us. . . . And that [means]
that the universe could not be static. . . .
but that it is in fact expanding . . .
growing all the time.

—Stephen W. Hawking

Rubber Band

I found it in the top
desk drawer, thick and red.
Place thumbs and middle fingers
together—17 inches—same as Scarlett's
waist that wound the whole romantic south:
Atlanta blushing and a dress hiding in drapery.
On the desk it falls into a figure 8. Picked up
from the middle, it fashions double loops like cells
dividing, repeating their simple selves into complexities
from that first red circle to the last pale O O O of the mouth.
In between, it's folded in, humming behind the pressed lips,
between the great doorposts of thigh, until their easy
eased opening of love answering ache and search and
find: the door, the slit, the wet necessity, the
swung gates of home, its roundly come space:
the elastic circle of strength, of stretch
that can rack and back-twist the spine
ratcheting the body on its own screw
on the wheel's blood-flecked clock
of hours until O the round
the red cry crowning.

Recovery

Little by little the body comes back,
the functions falling in orderly
as a shuffled deck. There's no pushing.
The body is patient as a rug.
Only the mind whines, circles its spot,
will not lie down. Even the saint,
cool in her whitewashed corner,
wrings her hands over her wound.

I examine the incision in the mirror, worry
the seepage lacing through like confession,
the line of the axe, its dizzy intrusion,
while the body (that old hod carrier)
goes about its business: walls and ramps,
the composition of structure, the blood
factory clicking in the bone.

Of the pale mind's fire—the diabolic
urge of the pen, the abracadabra to record
all snooty sensibilities of shock—the body
requires now only distraction,
as Hercules at the gates threw cakes
to the three-headed dog to still its yammering
when there was rescue to be done.

Turnip

Better to live
low, hide
beneath the purple
the bald white pubis.

Better to squat
in peace
after the boot
and November
obliterate the furrow.

Better
in an ocean of dirt
to let down anchor—
the rat's white cane
my long white pencil
that witchy root.

Invitation to a Minor Poet

Canadian Rockies

Here 70-foot pines clap short arms
like thalidomide kings
in the chinook winds. Here
the mountains wake in a face-off
with the sun and ride nights
motionless on the horns of Capricorn.
Here elk sniff, snort, threaten
then scratch their rumps
on a tree. Here is
imperial nonchalance—
the snow fields trailing off
Mt. Rundle's rocky back. And I
behind the glass of this safe
window in my stolen sweater—
the one I found and used for need
and kept for gratitude, like Claudius
warmed by the sin he was never sorry for—
wait for the lonely crescendo of each day
as if it were a play within a play
behind museum glass. Squirrels
chut-chut from the branches, waggling
the stubby fingers of the pines,
making invitation into a forgiving world
not that different from my own.
See, they say, the trees on the high
rocky face are like stubble
on a Sunday morning. Like Auden
you too can be at home in this world.

Letter to My Husband

Today through a low window
I looked at trunks of pine, cut off
oblivious to their tops. And I saw into
the lilac's naked cane beneath its flowering
where a bird came bursting color to its heart
and then I knew how each part
has a life and secret from the rest
without which the others could not
be: the hand won't reach for what the mouth
doesn't wet and yearn, for what the belly
has not hungered.
              And I write now to
remind you of the grocer's boy, opening
spring with strawberries and peas, the fall
in pyramids of pears. Who hefted grapes,
their heavy bubbles in his hands. Who
20 years ago on paper thrones balanced apples
and tins in towers at the aisle ends
and trimmed the greens.
              And I wanted you to know,
you whose struggle is to keep him dim
as his apron hung behind the door, as if
a flower could deny the green stem of its making
whose only job is sucking sweetness up. Oh,
Professor, it's the grocer's boy I lay me down
and his hopeful unsuspecting heart that leads me
through the storehouse of his hands—plums,
black cherries rumbling in the bin, hearts
of palm and artichoke, buttermilk and cream.

The Good News
for the mosquitoes of Minnesota

I managed to make them
very happy.
Whenever I went out
lilies opened on their pads
like satellite dishes
and butterflies
spread their flags
to flutter the good news. I was
the Red Cross rolling in
in a white truck—
donuts and blankets
sacks of rice & powdered
milk for the babies. I was
payday for the troops
R & R and a geisha
for Saturday nights, Lucky Strikes
and a kiss before dying.
I was the Berlin airlift
and the Marshall Plan—
chicken soup in vats
and a hunk of bread, ripped off
with the back teeth. I was
hope for the young
and succor for the old
and after me, surely
faith in a second coming
for it is I who answered
their wing & their prayer
who gathered to me
the whining dispirited
and unified the multitudes.
It is for me the cathedrals
for me the bells
for I am the miracle
the sacrificial lamb.

I am the staff of life
the bread basket of this world
the loaves and fishes
the body and the blood.

Archery Lesson

When they dug them up in Thessaloníki
the men were buried pointing west,
the women, east. Dressed for travel,
the splintered bone still wore
a best bracelet, the gold clasp at the waist.
The luggage too remained—boxes
of brass, a stash of silver and in filigree cases
all that is required: bronze greaves, necklaces of blue
glass, amber and shell.
Only the flesh was gone, shot like an arrow, east
or west, from its poor bone bow.

How we are drawn to these cases of last things
clustered around their bone, waiting for the flesh
to come back and fill in the spaces,
much as your shoes stand all a black night
empty, their usefulness yearning to be filled,
to be walked down any street once more
by your nocked and targeted flesh.

Light Years Away

The sun throws his triangle on the floor
then moves it clockwise
over the carpet, the registers,
the rocker's grinning feet, until he
hoists himself into the big chair
drapes his arms along its arms
leans back and laughs.

Think of all good things
come through glass—
light and heat and your blue eyes
and now this 10 a.m. inspector
fingering the asparagus fern
before he leaves.

What shall we do
now that we've earned this morning's
blaze? now that the sun
has chosen our big chair?

I say today we speak nothing
of nations. Today we add
and not divide. And if
in our small struggle, language
eases like light through a window,
forgiving in its drift the motes
inherent in one another's arms,

then could we not find the words
to whisper in the ear of the mystic
who waits, hunched over his Olivetti,
pecking out fortunes with one finger?

Would not his turban finally unwind?

Cherries

National Portrait Gallery, London

Catherine Hyde, Duchess of Queensberry,
beauty and wit, the favorite of Swift,
Congreve and Gay, still beautiful at 72,
died of a surfeit of cherries. (July 17, 1777)

1.
Captain Cook was clubbed
third voyage out. Sweet Anne Boleyn
lifted of her head. But Catherine Hyde
at home in the wit of compliance
the grace of enlightenment—of the
pearl grey and parasol, powdered
shoulders and the carefully
positioned patch—was

distillation of discretion
in the mirror of the silver pot.
Her ringed hand flew among porcelain
between creamer and cup
fluttering to punctuate
chat, then hover.
White dove over chaos.
Luminous principle
over the cherry bowl.

She should have died easy.
The swan's last
pillow on a lake

breath on a mirror
gathering itself off

or surrounded by wits
talking   talking
lace cuffs at the pillow
to the last.

2.

Whispers in the cherry bowl.
Whispers of a silk kimono
fallen by, the thigh
wrinkling on the bone
and days blank
as white asters
in a porcelain vase.

A lie a lie.

Whispers in the cherry bowl.
Cackle behind the fans. Excess.
Excess.
Byron's skulls and apes
and Shelley's heart. (Too early
too early) No nightingale
high-strung. Not yet the rales
resurrected into stars.

3.

No secret. Across
and down the blue parchment
her fine hand writes: *Joy.*
Oh my dear, yet it comes.
Joy of a morning. Iris spear
in sun shaft. Cherries and cream.
at   14   25   63
why should joy change?

Oh yes, there were lessons—sister
tearing through daisies
swinging legs in Papa's chair
magic pebbles in a reticule

then slipped into another skin
padded
like a winter cloak, grown up
and gone—
lost in a righteous pocket.

But fancy, me the small one.
My heart took all the room.
I danced to keep it beating.
Kitty they called me. Perched
on the clavier in a white dress.

Who knows how we choose?
I wrapped me in my youth
to live. Loosed the corset strings.
Ran in my hobbling hoops.
My breasts two apples in my hands.

But each July the orchard
moaned in its swag of cherries.
Mazzard. Double-flowered Morello.
Double saw-toothed leaves
and drooping. Shiny red. Night's
little black moons, two on a stem,
whispering on the same pillow,
the color of the inside of my mouth.
Cherries, we had been cherries
waiting for the sun to open
black to red—sisters
each big as a bite
the tongue's treasure
the mouth's rose   the whispering
stone
warm and round with blood.

4.
A girl dances through her days
dances up to meet her sadness
writes its name in her tasseled book
curtsies
takes the white-gloved hand.

A girl hums in her bed at night
learns to listen to what grows
swallows down her portion
then eats from what she used to love
handfuls
getting it all down.

Night Drive

Tonight the trees are tossing the clouds around
and the moon in her wedge of white make-up
leans back to hold us in her spotlight of hair.
A dog barks. A garage door lowers and locks.
And every building freezes for the portrait of the world.

Where is defeat on such a night as this?
Each pebble on the side of the road
shouts a victory in the flash of my headlights,
for I have come to the end of fifty-five years,
each one the eraser for the last, each one
a newly sharpened pencil jabbing me awake
to this picture—here and hung—on this night's black wall.

And I am driving, driving for Jimmy Wonderland
down the white line of my own intentions,
glancing in the rear-view mirror with a stone's cold eye.
And I know I have never been here before
for I've thrown the old key out the car window to lie
in a ditch somewhere in a broken spill of trash—its crockery,
its egg shells, its unloved dolly clutching at the dirt.

Imagine what you like: say this film
is a loop played round and before, or that I drive
a winding hill passing the same sign on repeated rights.
But it is night. The dark surrounds, presses, then
slides off. I *see* no sign but this white immediacy
quickening in the brights of my car. And nowhere
beyond the reach of my eyes is more sweet than here
when marrow blooms in the bone and starts to speak.

About the Author

Alice Friman, born in New York City, has lived in Indianapolis since 1960. She attended Brooklyn College and Butler University and is Professor Emerita of English at the University of Indianapolis. The author of *Reporting from Corinth* and four chapbooks, she is the winner of the Award for Excellence in Poetry from *Hopewell Review*, 1995, Japan's *Abiko Quarterly* International Poetry Contest, 1994, and three prizes from Poetry Society of America. Her poems have appeared in *Poetry, Georgia Review, Gettysburg Review, Shenandoah, Manoa,* and publications in seven other countries. In 1996 she received an Individual Artist Fellowship from the Indiana Arts Commission.

INVERTED FIRE

Alice Friman

Photo by Lillian Elaine Wilson

ALICE FRIMAN, born in New York City, has lived in Indianapolis, Indiana, since 1960. She is the author of *Zoo*, winner of the 1998 Ezra Pound Poetry Award, *Reporting from Corinth* (Barnwood Press 1984), and four chapbooks. Her poems have appeared in *Poetry, Shenandoah, Georgia Review, Gettysburg Review, Manoa*, among many others, including publications in seven other countries. Her numerous awards include the Award for Excellence in Poetry from *Hopewell Review*, 1995; Japan's *Abiko Quarterly* International Poetry Contest, 1994; and three prizes from the Poetry Society of America. She has performed readings of her poetry across the United States and in Australia. She is Professor Emerita of English at the University of Indianapolis.

"Alice Friman's poems are among the finest contemporary poetry has to offer—sustaining the dramatic language of a 'wildness that burns,' cupping that fierce song in graceful forms that hold and heal like lullabies. Here is the embodiment of 'truth and beauty'—form and content melded in a 'balance for weighing the soul.' Myth and lyric married, all affectation spurned, idiomatic speech rides elegiac rhythms. For those who love poetry, this is *home.*"
—*MARILYN KALLET*

"These poems asseverate that life is larger than particulars, and that what it means and why it matters depend on us. *Inverted Fire* finds its way beyond an often numbing sense of danger and inevitable loss to the belief that, 'like Auden [we] too can be at home in the world.'"
—*INDIANA REVIEW*

"Alice Friman's sensuous poems edify, surprise, and amuse. She is a poet who can capture the pain of loss and chart and route recovery with equal skill. Read."
—*DIANA DER-HOVANESSIAN*
NOMINATED FOR A
1997 NATIONAL BOOK AWARD

B k M k **PRESS**
THE UNIVERSITY OF MISSOURI—KANSAS CITY

ISBN 1-886157-07-3
51195
9 781886 157071